Rally Cars

BY DENNY VON FINN

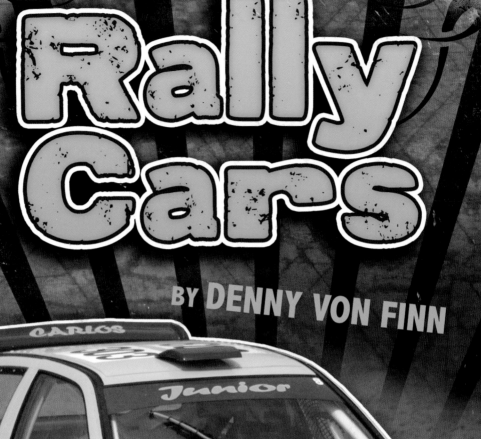

BELLWETHER MEDIA • MINNEAPOLIS, MN

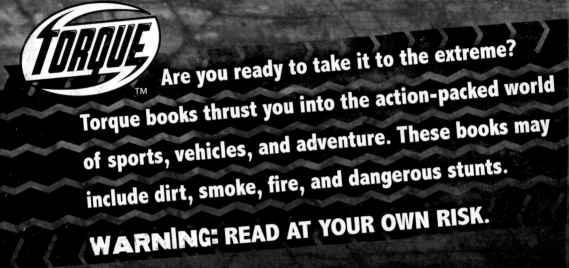

Are you ready to take it to the extreme? Torque books thrust you into the action-packed world of sports, vehicles, and adventure. These books may include dirt, smoke, fire, and dangerous stunts.

WARNING: READ AT YOUR OWN RISK.

This edition first published in 2009 by Bellwether Media.

No part of this publication may be reproduced in whole or in part without written permission of the publisher. For information regarding permission, write to Bellwether Media Inc., Attention: Permissions Department, Post Office Box 19349, Minneapolis, MN 55419.

Library of Congress Cataloging-in-Publication Data
Von Finn, Denny.
  Rally cars / by Denny Von Finn.
    p. cm. — (Torque : cool rides)
  Includes bibliographical references and index.
  Summary: "Amazing photography accompanies engaging information about rally cars. The combination of high-interest subject matter and light text is intended for readers in grades 3 through 7"—Provided by publisher.
  ISBN-13: 978-1-60014-212-3 (hardcover : alk. paper)
  ISBN-10: 1-60014-212-5 (hardcover : alk. paper)
  1. Automobiles, Racing—Juvenile literature. 2. Automobiles, Racing—Pictorial works—Juvenile literature. 3. Automobile rallies—Juvenile literature. 4. Automobile rallies—Pictorial works—Juvenile literature. I. Title.

TL236.V66 2009
629.228—dc22   2008017020

Contents

What Is a Rally Car?

Rally cars look like normal cars on the road. However, they have many special features to help meet the tough demands of a **rally**.

Drivers race on public roads. The roads are closed to other motorists during a rally. Hundreds of fans watch from the roadside! The cars slide along mountain cliffs and cruise over muddy forest trails. They may even drive over snow, ice, and sand. Rally cars must be prepared for long, tough races.

Rally Car History

Rallies began more than one hundred years ago. Drivers raced their cars from city to city. By 1940, some rallies were several thousand miles long! Automakers used these races to promote their cars.

Until the 1950s, most rally cars were normal cars. People didn't have to buy special cars or special parts. This helped rallying become popular.

In the 1960s, automakers began building cars designed for rallying. It became expensive to buy rally cars. Still, the sport remained popular. It is a favorite form of racing in Europe. In the United States, it is growing in popularity.

Fast FaCt

The World Rally Championship (WRC) is the most famous rally series. Each WRC race season includes rallies on five continents.

Parts of a Rally Car

Rally cars have many parts to help them on rally courses. Rally cars have **four-wheel drive**. The engine turns all four wheels. This helps the tires grip any kind of terrain. Special tires with metal studs are used on snowy and icy rally courses. A **suspension system** connects the wheels and tires to a strong **chassis**.

Together, the suspension system and chassis aid a rally car on uneven and slippery surfaces. Rally cars can even become airborne on very bumpy courses. The strong chassis helps the cars withstand these jumps.

Top rally cars are equipped with
turbochargers. These devices increase the
engine's **horsepower**. Powerful engines
and challenging terrain are a dangerous
combination. Rally cars can roll over when
they jump over hills or drift around corners.
A **rollcage** protects the driver and **co-driver**
in case of a rollover.

Rally Cars in Action

A rally course can be several hundred miles long. A course is divided into **stages** and can take days to complete. Each stage is timed. The drivers begin each stage alone. This way, the cars won't crash into each other during the race. With trees, cliffs, houses, and even people alongside the course, there is no room for error.

Rally cars are driven from one stage to the next in public traffic. For this reason, rally cars must be **street-legal**.

Rallies take place in all kinds of weather during all times of day. They are never canceled because of bad weather. Some stages are even held at night. This kind of racing is intense.

Fast Fact

Rally America's RC Championship series features several races around the United States each year.

One key to success is the co-driver. The co-driver sits in the passenger seat and calls out **pace notes**. These instructions let the driver know ahead of time which way to turn and what to expect on the road.

Fast FaCt

Rallying is extremely popular in northern Europe. Drivers from that part of the world won 16 of the first 31 WRC Driver's Championships.

Every stage has new challenges. A rally course is much too complex for one driver to handle. It takes teamwork to win the race.

Glossary

chassis—the metal frame of an automobile

co-driver—the racer who sits in the rally car's passenger seat and calls out instructions to the driver

four-wheel drive—a system in which the engine provides power to all four of a vehicle's wheels

horsepower—a unit for measuring the power of an engine

pace notes—a detailed course description that the co-driver reads to the driver through an intercom during a rally

rally—a point-to-point automobile race held on public roadways of asphalt, gravel, mud, sand, snow, or ice

rollcage—a set of strong metal bars that protect the driver and co-driver in case of a rollover

stage—a timed segment of a rally course

street-legal—able to legally be driven on public roads

suspension system—a series of springs and shock absorbers that connect the chassis of a vehicle to its wheels

turbocharger—a device that forces air into an engine, allowing more fuel to enter the engine, which creates more power

To Learn More

AT THE LIBRARY

Braulick, Carrie A. *Rally Cars*. Mankato, Minn.: Capstone, 2007.

Savage, Jeff. *Rally Cars*. Mankato, Minn.: Capstone, 2004.

Stephenson, Sallie. *Rally Racing*. Mankato, Minn.: Crestwood House, 1991.

ON THE WEB

Learning more about rally cars

is as easy as 1, 2, 3.

1. Go to www.factsurfer.com

2. Enter "rally cars" into search box.

3. Click the "Surf" button and you will
   see a list of related web sites.

With factsurfer.com, finding more information is just a click away.

Index

The images in this book are reproduced through the courtesy of: Marcel Jancovic, front cover; Les Kolczak, pp. 4-5, 6, 7, 12, 14, 15, 17 (top, bottom), 18, pp. 20-21; Marka / agefotostock, pp. 8-9; Quinn / Getty Images, pp. 10-11; Luis Louro, p. 13; Sally Ann Baines / Alamy, p. 19.